LINDA BOZZO

Amazing Animal Tongues

PowerKiDS press.

New York

To my family and friends and all of your amazing features that make you who you are.
—LBS

Published in 2008 by The Rosen Publishing Group, Inc.
29 East 21st Street, New York, NY 10010

Copyright © 2008 by The Rosen Publishing Group, Inc.

All rights reserved. No part of this book may be reproduced in any form without permission in writing from the publisher, except by a reviewer.

First Edition

Editor: Joanne Randolph
Book Design: Kate Laczynski
Photo Researcher: Nicole Pristash

Photo Credits: Cover, p. 13 © Superstock.com; p. 5 © Roland Seitre/Peter Arnold, Inc.; p. 7 © Heinz Plenge/Peter Arnold, Inc.; pp. 9, 11, 19, 21 Shutterstock.com; p. 15 © Ed Reschke/Peter Arnold, Inc.; p. 17 © Rauschenbach, F./Peter Arnold, Inc.

Library of Congress Cataloging-in-Publication Data

Bozzo, Linda.
  Amazing animal tongues / Linda Bozzo. — 1st ed.
      p. cm. — (Creature features)
  Includes index.
  ISBN 978-1-4042-4172-5 (library binding)
  1. Tongue—Juvenile literature. I. Title.

QL946.B69 2008
591.4'3—dc22

                                    2007033531

Manufactured in the United States of America

CONTENTS

Open Wide 4

Sticky Tongues 6

Busy Bee 8

Like a Straw 10

Zap That! 12

A Taste-Bud Body 14

In a Flash 16

A Really Long Tongue 18

A Tongue That's a Nose 20

Look It Over 22

Glossary 23

Index 24

Web Sites.........................24

Open wide! You will likely find a tongue inside most animals' mouths. The tongue is best known for taking food in. The tongue of some animals is perfect for what they eat. There are tongues that are sticky. Sticky tongues are great for catching bugs. Other tongues are very long. Long tongues can reach places that other tongues cannot.

Many animals use their tongue for things besides eating, too. For example, a snake uses its tongue to smell. Different animals' tongues have to be different because animals live in all sorts of **habitats**.

When in danger, Australia's blue-tongue lizard opens its mouth wide and sticks out its tongue. Its bright blue tongue scares enemies away.

STICKY TONGUES

Anteaters are known for their long, tube-shaped head and their long tongue. An anteater uses its sharp claws to tear open ant or termite hills. It sticks its long tongue down into the nests of its **prey**. These little bugs do not have much time to escape. The anteater moves its tongue in and out of the nest very quickly.

A hungry anteater can dine on a few thousand bugs in just a few short minutes. What is this animal's secret? The anteater can trap its prey on its sticky tongue. Yum!

A giant anteater's tongue is about 2 feet (60 cm) long. It is covered in tiny spines, or points, which help it catch and hold its dinner.

BUSY BEE

You have probably seen a yellow and black bug flying around your garden. This busy neighbor is likely the honeybee. The honeybee has a long tongue called a **proboscis**. On the end of the proboscis is a spoon-shaped part called the glossa.

The proboscis looks like a simple tube, but it is a very important tool. The bee reaches deep inside flowers with its proboscis. Then it uses the **glossa** to sip **nectar**. The bee stores the nectar and returns to the nest. This sweet liquid will be turned into honey. Now that is one very busy bee!

This honeybee dips its proboscis into a flower. The bee will pass the nectar it drinks to another bee, which will hold the nectar on its tongue until the water evaporates, or leaves.

Bees are not the only bugs with a proboscis. A butterfly flies from flower to flower looking for nectar. Nectar is the chief food of most butterflies. An adult butterfly cannot bite or chew. When it finds nectar, it unrolls its long, thin tongue, or proboscis. Like a straw, the butterfly uses the proboscis to suck the sweet nectar from the flower. When the butterfly is done eating, it rolls the proboscis back up.

Believe it or not, butterflies do not taste with their tongue. They taste with their feet and legs instead.

This butterfly's proboscis is the part that is curled up on its head. The proboscis has a sharp tip, which the butterfly can use to cut into fruits or to reach into flowers.

ZAP THAT!

When you think of great hunters, what animals do you think of? You likely think of lions, wolves, and sharks. Chameleons are unlikely to be on your list. Chameleons are great hunters, though. What is their secret? Chameleons have a long tongue that moves quickly.

A chameleon's tongue is sometimes longer than the lizard's body. When a chameleon sees a tasty bug, it creeps up on its prey. The chameleon's long tongue shoots out. Zap! The bug is caught on the sticky tip of the lizard's tongue. The tongue snaps back, pulling dinner into the chameleon's mouth. Gulp!

This chameleon has caught a tasty grasshopper with its sticky tongue. When a chameleon's tongue is not being used, it folds up into the lizard's mouth.

A TASTE-BUD BODY

An earthworm does not breathe through a mouth or a nose. Believe it or not, an earthworm breathes through its skin. What is even more amazing is that the earthworm's whole body is like one big tongue. The earthworm's body is covered with taste buds. These taste buds are called **chemoreceptors**.

These chemoreceptors allow the earthworm to taste and smell. This is how it is able to find food. Earthworms eat as they dig through the soil. They are a very important part of the soil habitat. Without earthworms, plants would not grow well. Many animals **depend** on earthworms, too.

Earthworms can be anywhere from less than 1 inch (2 cm) to nearly 10 feet (3 m) long. Imagine a 10-foot- (3 m) long tongue! That is a mouthful!

A fly buzzes past, but suddenly it disappears. What happened? Maybe a frog or toad snapped it up. Some frogs and toads use their tongue to catch bugs. These frogs and toads have their tongue at the front of their mouth. This **feature** lets the frog or toad reach bugs more easily.

The frog or toad will wait for a yummy bug to pass by. While it waits, its tongue is folded up inside its mouth. The end of the tongue points toward the throat. Then it flips its long, sticky tongue out to nab its prey.

This frog has caught a fly on its sticky tongue. It will swallow the fly in one piece since it has teeth only on the top part of its mouth.

A REALLY LONG TONGUE

Giraffes have a tongue that is **prehensile**. This means that a giraffe can put its tongue around branches. A prehensile tongue helps the giraffe strip leaves off trees so it can eat them. With its long tongue, the giraffe can pull off only a few leaves at a time. This means that this large animal spends most of its day eating. A giraffe needs a lot of food!

A giraffe's tongue is up to 20 inches (50 cm) long, and it is bluish black. The dark color of the giraffe's tongue is thought to keep it from getting sunburned.

This giraffe stretches out its long tongue to pull a few leaves from the tree. A giraffe may eat up to 75 pounds (34 kg) of leaves each day.

A snake's tongue darts in and out of its mouth. The snake is not being mean. It smells the air with its tongue. It is true. Snakes can smell with their nose but that is not enough. The snake's tongue tells the snake even more about the smells around it.

When the snake sticks its tongue out, it takes in small bits of smell from the air or anything it touches. The next time a snake sticks its tongue out at you, remember, it is just smelling you.

Do you see the fork at the end of this snake's tongue? The fork helps the snake tell from which direction a smell is coming.

The world we live in changes all the time. Animals must change, too. An animal's tongue is just one special feature that must **adapt**. If animals did not adapt to where they lived, they would die. There are many jobs that tongues are made to do. Some are adapted to help an animal find food, like the snake's tongue does. Others are adapted to catch prey, like a frog's tongue does.

The next time an animal sticks out its tongue, look it over carefully. You might just be amazed at what you see.

adapt (uh-DAPT) To change to fit requirements.

chemoreceptors (kee-moh-rih-SEP-turz) Body parts used to smell and taste.

depend (dih-PEND) To count on.

feature (FEE-chur) The special look or form of a person, an animal, or an object.

glossa (GLOS-uh) The tongue in an insect, such as a bee.

habitats (HA-beh-tats) The kinds of land where animals or plants naturally live.

nectar (NEK-tur) A sweet liquid found in flowers.

prehensile (pree-HEN-sul) Able to hold on by curling around.

prey (PRAY) An animal that is hunted by another animal for food.

proboscis (pruh-BAH-sus) A tubelike mouthpart that bugs use to suck in liquid food.

INDEX

A
anteater(s), 6

B
bug(s), 6, 12, 16
butterfly, 10

C
chameleon(s), 12
chemoreceptors, 14

E
earthworm(s), 14

F
feature, 16, 22
frog(s), 16, 22

G
giraffe(s), 18
glossa, 8

N
nectar, 8, 10

P
prey, 6, 12, 16, 22
proboscis, 8, 10

S
snake(s), 4, 20
soil, 14

WEB SITES

Due to the changing nature of Internet links, PowerKids Press has developed an online list of Web sites related to the subject of this book. This site is updated regularly. Please use this link to access the list:

www.powerkidslinks.com/cfeat/tongue/